BACKPACKER

The Magazine Of Wilderness Travel

ADVENTURE JOURNAL

A Note to the Writer

I'm no Hemingway. I'm no Van Gogh. In fact, if I'm being totally honest, some of the stick figure drawings my son brings home from preschool are far more interesting than anything I can do. But there's one thing I've learned from years of taking wilderness trips: it's better to come home with a notebook filled with doodles and chicken scratch than to finish a trip empty-handed.

The key, I think, to keeping a satisfying journal is to simply loosen up. Just start scribbling. Forget about trying to document every turn in the trail, every gorgeous vista, every hour of every day of your trip. (Though writing about the former two can be very rewarding.) Just write something. Draw something—I've included some sketches. If you dare, paint something. Don't let the blank pages intimidate you and don't worry about crafting perfect complete sentences, unless you're in the mood to do so. "Stream of consciousness" writing is very therapeutic and fun to read. Sentence fragments, contrary to what your tenth grade English teacher said, are perfectly acceptable. Spelling mistakes? Who cares!

This book is designed to make keeping a journal easier. You'll find plenty of blank pages for writing and drawing, plus a long list of potential topics to choose from in case you hit writer's block. There are also lots of helpful tips so you can bone up on your outdoor skills. But the majority of this text will come from you. This book is a blank canvas. Only you can transform it into a masterpiece.

As for supplies, pack a pencil with eraser and a ballpoint pen (which won't smudge or run if a raindrop hits the page). If you want to try watercolors, check an art supply store for small, packable kits that come in hard plastic containers. Stash all your supplies in a zipper-lock bag, and don't bury the bag at the bottom of your pack where it will be forgotten.

The bottom line: Whether you're doing it for your own eyes only or you plan on sharing your musings with someone back home, it matters not. With a little effort, this journal and the others that will follow when this one is brimming will become the most treasured souvenirs of your trips.

—Kristin Hostetter, Contributor, *Backpacker* magazine

Need some tips getting started? Check these out:

- Write about the best and worst things that happened to you in the last twenty-four hours. Think beyond the pretty things you see. Your best and worst moments could be a fantastic meal, a great conversation, jumping into a lovely lake, a lung-busting climb, a moment of panic, or simply crawling into your sleeping bag with a hot water bottle at the end of the day.
- Make time to work in your journal. It's easy to tell yourself the day is too hectic (too many miles to hike, dinner to cook, dishes to do, water to pump, tents to set up, etc.) to journal. But crazy days make for the best journal entries! Whether it's a few sleepy minutes in your bag at night, a quiet sunrise session with a cup of java, or a midday snack break, jot down something that reflects your day.
- Try to keep things varied. Maybe you want to fill some pages with words, but try mixing things up, too. No need to always write horizontally across the page. Try writing diagonally or tilt the book sideways and write across the long side. Draw little symbols that reflect the weather, such as  for sunny skies,  for overcast,  for rain,  for snow.
- To jazz up a page, try the occasional list. An example from an all-girls trip: THINGS GIRLS DO WHEN BOYS AREN'T AROUND: 1) fish; 2) drink scotch; 3) play chess; 4) give everything a name (as in "Scottie" for the bottle of scotch); 5) spin tales; 6) relax; and 7) curse.
- Try your hand at poetry, even if it's only a goofy limerick. You and your hiking buddies might come up with these as you stroll down the trail; record them for posterity.

  I once knew a boy who wore black hiking socks
  Though fashion impaired, he ate like an ox.
  When his food bag ran dry,
  He backtracked on the fly,
  Found a deli with bagels and lox.

- Need some help with inspiring words? Try some of these: awe-inspiring, awesome, balanced, beautiful, breathtaking, calm, charming, clear, dazzling, delicate, delightful, dignified, divine, elegant, ethereal, exhilarating, exquisite, glittering, glorious, graceful, grand, great, harmonious, heavenly, imposing, impressive, inspiring, invigorating, limpid, magnificent, majestic, noble, peaceful, perfect, radiant, refreshing, regal, resplendent, rousing, sacred, serene, simple, spectacular, splendid, stirring, sublime, tranquil, undisturbed, uplifting, wonderful, wondrous.

Date . . . . Mileage . . . .

>> If you could go anywhere in the world, where would you go?

Location

Date . . . . Mileage . . . .

[tip] Always stake your tent, even if there's nary a breeze. Staking maximizes interior space and prevents leaks should the rain kick up. Plus, you never know when a gust of wind could blow your investment away like a cheap kite.

Location . . . .

Date . . . . Mileage . . . .

[tip] Don't let bad weather inhibit your photography. Rain seems to heighten colors, and sometimes features are crystal clear when the sky is overcast. Try to include something colorful in your photo, like a person in bright clothing.

Location

Date . . . . **Mileage** . . . .

Location . . . .

Date . . . . **Mileage** . . . .

>> Hello, bear! Had any exciting wildlife encounters?

Location

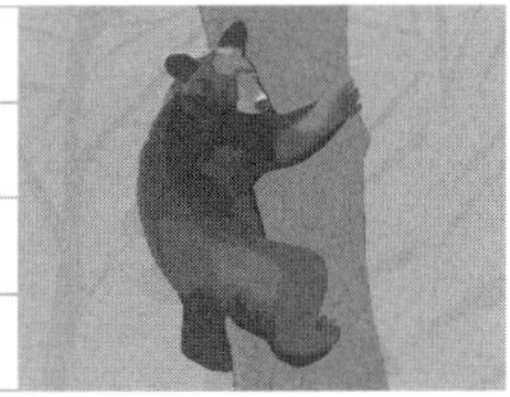

Date . . . . **Mileage** . . . .

Location . . . .

[tip] Don't let the bugs bug you. If the storm risk is low, make camp on a high, open ridge where breezes will blow pesky biters away. If they do find your camp, a DEET-based repellant is the most effective way to keep them from biting, though some people find natural concoctions (i.e. citronella) work fine in mildly buggy conditions.

Date . . . . Mileage . . . .

Location

Date . . . . Mileage . . . .

[tip] When winter camping, stomp out a flat tent-wide spot in the snow with your skis, snowshoes, or boots. Then let it harden for about half an hour before setting up your tent. Otherwise, you'll be tossing and turning on lumpy snow all night.

Location . . . .

Date . . . . **Mileage** . . . .

>> What foods (or beverages) are you craving? Did any meals win "worst campfood" awards? Learn any meal ideas from others?

Location

Date . . . . Mileage . . . .

[tip] Don't develop a drinking problem. Make sure your water bottle is easy to reach all day long to avoid dehydration. You should consume 4 to 6 quarts per day and even more in high altitudes or in the desert.

Location . . . .

Date . . . . **Mileage** . . . .

Location

[tip] Air your bag. As soon as you crawl out of it in the morning, fluff your bag then string it up somewhere while you breakfast and pack. This freshens it up a bit and allows any built-up moisture to evaporate.

Date . . . . **Mileage** . . . .

Location . . . .

Date . . . . **Mileage** . . . .

Location

Date . . . . **Mileage** . . . .

Location . . . .

[tip] If your clothes get wet, change into dry ones at the end of the day, then spread out the wet ones inside your bag at night. Your body heat will dry them by morning (assuming the clothes are synthetic and that they are not sopping wet to start out with).

Date . . . . Mileage . . . .

[tip] Testing 1, 2, 3. Always try new gear (set up tents, fire up new stoves) before you head out. If you've loaned your gear since your last trip, make sure it still works.

Location

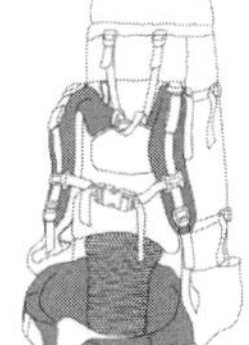

Date . . . . **Mileage** . . . .

Location . . . .

Date . . . . Mileage . . . .

>> What's the most beautiful thing you've experienced so far?

Location

Date . . . . Mileage . . . .

[tip] Don't dry your boots near the fire—they'll shrink! Remove the insoles, loosen the laces, and stow them inside your tent near the foot of your sleeping bag.

Location . . . .

Date . . . . Mileage . . . .

Location

Date . . . . **Mileage** . . . .

Location . . . .

[tip] Greet the sun. Orient your tent door to the east, to face the rising sun. In the evening you can stroll away from your tent to catch the sunset, but you'll appreciate those cheery, warming rays in the chill of the new day.

Date . . . . **Mileage** . . . .

>> Weather affecting your mood, itinerary, gear, comfort, and your trip?

Location

Date . . . . Mileage . . . .

[tip] Stuff, don't roll. When packing your tent, bag, or clothes, cram them straight into the stuff sack to optimize space.

Location . . . .

Date . . . . **Mileage** . . . .

Location

[tip] Keep your toenails trimmed, but not too short. Long nails can wear out socks and crack under downhill pressure. Too-short nails don't provide enough support for the ends of your toes and may grow into your skin, becoming painful ingrown toenails.

Date . . . . **Mileage** . . . .

Location . . . .

Date . . . . Mileage . . . .

>> Have you had any epiphanies about your "real" life back home? Things you want to do, or do better, or stop doing?

Location

Date . . . . **Mileage** . . . .

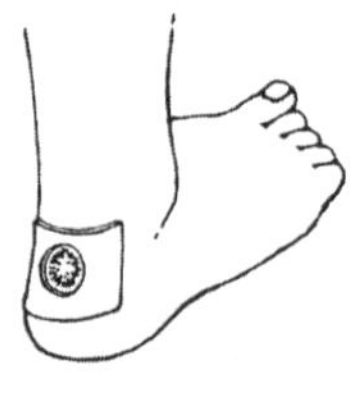

Location . . . .

[tip] Restock your first-aid kit when you return home. Make sure you replace the bandages, painkillers, and moleskin you used on that last trip.

Date . . . . **Mileage** . . . .

Location

Date . . . . **Mileage** . . . .

[tip] When camping in grizzly country, establish a triangular campsite. Tent at one point, kitchen at another, and food storage at the third. Each area should be at least 100 yards from the rest.

Location

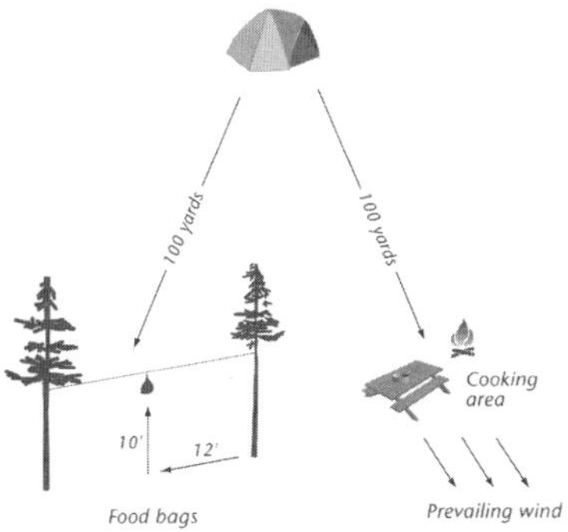

100 yards
100 yards
Cooking area
10'
12'
Food bags
Prevailing wind

Date . . . . Mileage . . . .

>> Wonderful water. Have you come across a particularly tasty, cold creek or a refreshing swimming hole?

Location

Date . . . . Mileage . . . .

[tip] Wash your hands. Be religious about this, especially after a bowel movement. It's the best way to keep you and your companions germ-free.

Location . . . .

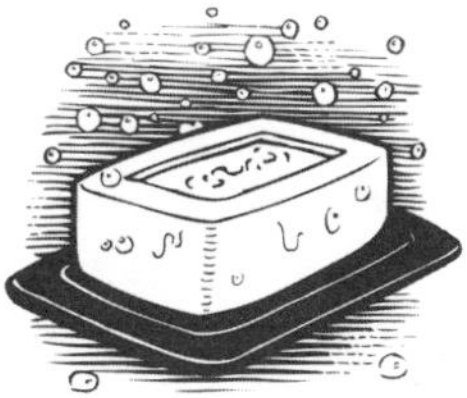

Date . . . . Mileage . . . .

Location

Date . . . . Mileage . . . .

Location . . . .

Date . . . . Mileage . . . .

>> There once was a . . .

Location

Date . . . . **Mileage** . . . .

Location . . . .

[tip] If your trip entails lots of stream crossings, paddling, rafting, or any extended encounters with water, pack a pair of lightweight sandals to change into so your boots stay dry.

Date . . . . **Mileage** . . . .

Location

Date . . . . Mileage . . . .

[tip] If you're not having fun, you're doing something wrong. Re-evaluate. A wilderness trip is a terrible thing to waste.

Location . . . .

Date . . . . **Mileage** . . . .

>> Seen any colorful wildflowers on this trip?

Location

[tip] Make a computer printout of a detailed packing list and keep it taped to the wall near your gear. No more forgotten batteries!

Date . . . . **Mileage** . . . .

Location . . . .

Date . . . . Mileage . . . .

Location

Date . . . . **Mileage** . . . .

[tip] Always cover your pot when boiling water. The water will boil more quickly this way, saving fuel.

Location . . . .

Date . . . . Mileage . . . .

>> Gear: A love/hate relationship. What's the worst gear malfunction you've ever had?

Location . . . .

Date . . . . Mileage . . . .

[tip] Select the right "pajamas." Opt for just one layer of clothing (your long johns or shorts and tee shirt) when tucking in at night. Too many clothes can compress your bag's insulation and create cold spots. And sleeping naked leaves dirt and oils on your bag's liner, which isn't healthy for you or your bag.

Location . . . .

Date . . . . Mileage . . . .

[tip] Bring at least 30 feet of thin parachute cord. You'll use it for hanging your food from trees, repairing your gear, fashioning a clothesline, and a thousand other things.

Location

Date . . . . **Mileage** . . . .

Location . . . .

Date . . . . **Mileage** . . . .

>> What games have you and your comrades played or invented?

Location

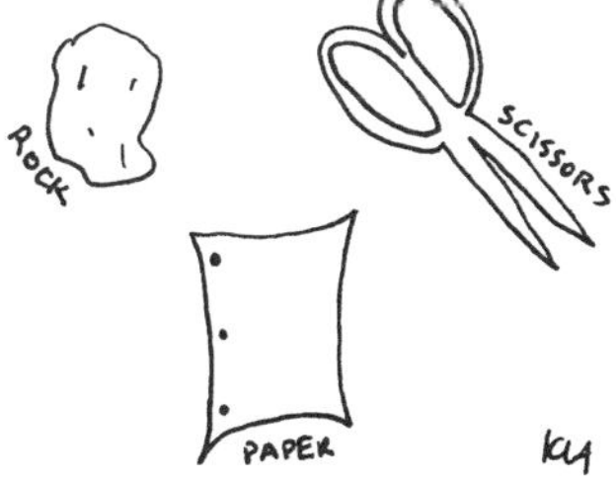

Date . . . . Mileage . . . .

Location . . . .

[tip] Take every opportunity to swim, assuming it's not forty below. It will revitalize, clean, and invigorate you.

Date . . . . **Mileage** . . . .

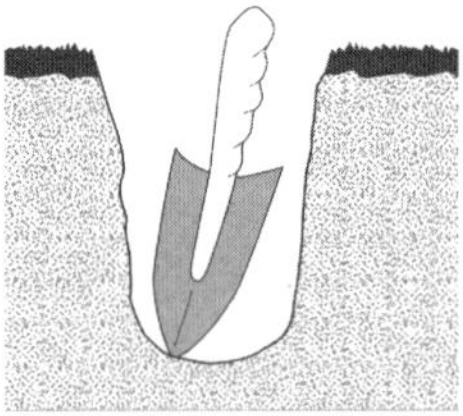

Location

[tip] Practice Leave No Trace. Take a few extra minutes to scour your campsite for forgotten bits of trash before you hit the trail.

Date . . . . **Mileage** . . . .

Location . . . .

Date . . . . Mileage . . . .

>> Missing someone? Write a passionate letter to a loved one back home. You don't have to mail it!

Location

Date . . . . Mileage . . . .

[tip] Snuggle up with something warm. Fill a wide-mouthed, leakproof water bottle with a hot drink at bedtime and slip it into a "bottle cozy." You'll sleep warmer at night, plus wake up to a warm drink.

Location . . . .

Date . . . . Mileage . . . .

Location

Date . . . . **Mileage** . . . .

Location . . . .

[tip] Add a few tablespoons of dried milk to your cocoa to make it taste creamier.

Date . . . . **Mileage** . . . .

>> Litterbugs, loud Larrys, mooches—
had any experiences with these types?

Location

Date . . . . Mileage . . . .

[tip] Customize your maps. When you find the perfect campsite or swimming hole, mark the area on your map with a pencil or highlighter so you'll be sure to find it next time.

Location

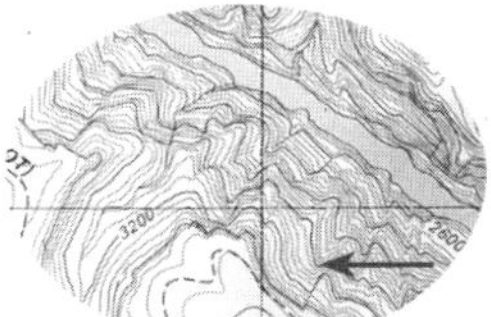

Date . . . . **Mileage** . . . .

Location

Date . . . . **Mileage** . . . .

Location . . . .

[tip] Make a point to try at least one new recipe on each trip. Search online or pick up a camp cookbook and chef up something tasty on your next trip.

Date . . . . **Mileage** . . . .

>> What are the dynamics of your group?

Location

Date . . . . **Mileage** . . . .

[tip] Zipper-lock bags are a hiker's best friend. Use them to protect food, clothes, and maps.

Location . . . .

Date . . . . Mileage . . . .

[tip] Go to bed with something in your belly, and it'll warm you from the inside out. In winter an empty stomach almost always promises a cold night in your bag.

Location

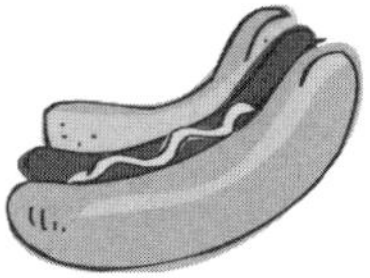

Date . . . . Mileage . . . .

Location . . . .

Date **Mileage**

>> If you could take a camping trip with anyone in the world, who would it be?

Location

After a long soak in the creek, a wet Dixie retired to the coolness of the tent and the fluffiness of our bags.

Date . . . . **Mileage** . . . .

[tip] In winter, wear black. It absorbs sunlight and will keep you warmer. In the heat, wear white, for the exact opposite reason.

Location . . . .

Date . . . . Mileage . . . .

Location

[tip] Keep an emergency set of dry socks in a zipper-lock bag. Stow them in your sleeping bag for nighttime and emergency use only.

Date . . . . **Mileage** . . . .

Location . . . .

Date

Mileage

>> Each trip is a learning experience. What will you take away from this trip?

Location

Date . . . . **Mileage** . . . .

[tip] In cool weather, wear a hat to bed to help conserve body heat during the night.

Location

Date Mileage

Location

Date . . . . **Mileage** . . . .

[tip] Wrap some duct tape around your water bottle, trekking pole, or flashlight handle so you'll always have a strip handy for a quick repair.

Location . . . .

Date Mileage

>> Years from now your ancestors will want to know about your passion for the outdoors. How about leaving a readable time capsule, including vivid descriptions of your favorite hikes, pieces of gear, backcountry meals, and so forth?

Location

Dedication

For Annie, whose journals are gold

How I Became a Journaler

I have always had respect for people who keep journals. And as a person who makes her living writing for publications, I've been ashamed at my pitiful journaling attempts. Journaling takes discipline. It takes commitment. It takes time, which I never seem to have enough of. For years I made all sorts of excuses for not keeping a journal of my expeditions. I convinced myself that my journals would be boring and pointless. People who keep journals, I'd tell myself, are the smart ones. They're the ones with brilliant observations, profound thoughts, and a distinct eye for everything that matters. I have none of those things. Or so I thought.

It took ten years of trip taking, then ten days in the Alaska bush for me to loosen up enough to give journaling a concerted effort. I was with my friend, Annie, who has always kept the most amazing journals. Each page is crammed full of her lovely, legible penmanship and sprinkled with line drawings, poetry, symbols, arrows, squigglies, and hand-drawn borders. She writes about everything: the beautiful things, the ugly things, the funny things, the scary things, the delicious things, the disgusting things, the happy things, the sad things.

On this particular day, we were wandering through a sunny expanse of tundra flat. The groundcover was a mosaic of gold, green, and red—tiny, rugged little plants thick as a shag carpet. In the distance a glimmer of white caught my eye. As we got closer we recognized the curvaceous, bleached form of a giant moose antler. Annie immediately whipped out her watercolors and settled in to paint. The scooped-out shape of the antler was a bit too intimidating for me, so I chose a 5-inch sprig of the Christmas-colored tundra. I carefully sketched the stalk and the serrated leaves with a pencil, then began mixing the paints. It only took about half an hour, and when I was finished, I was mighty proud. My masterpiece (it's the painting screened behind this text!). On the pages that followed, I wrote about the way the sun warmed my scalp as I sat in the moss.

Now, five years later, when I open up that journal I can still smell the fresh Alaska air, taste the blueberry pancakes we ate for breakfast, and feel that warm sun in my hair. Without my journal, it would all be another hazy memory.

—Kristin Hostetter

THE MOUNTAINEERS BOOKS
is the nonprofit publishing arm of The Mountaineers Club,
an organization founded in 1906 and dedicated to the exploration,
preservation, and enjoyment of outdoor and wilderness areas.

1001 SW Klickitat Way, Suite 201, Seattle, Washington, 98134

BACKPACKER
The Magazine Of Wilderness Travel
33 East Minor Street
Emmaus, PA 18098
800-666-3434
www.backpacker.com

The mission of *Backpacker* magazine is to provide accurate, useful, in-depth, and engaging information about wilderness recreation in North America.

First edition, 2004

Published simultaneously in Great Britain by Cordee, 3a DeMontfort Street, Leicester, England, LE1 7HD

Manufactured in China

Developmental Editor: Cassandra Conyers
Project Editor: Kathleen Cubley
Cover, Book Design, and Layout: Mayumi Thompson

A Note About Safety

Safety is an important concern in all outdoor activities. No book can alert you to every hazard or anticipate the limitations of every reader. The descriptions of techniques and procedures in this book are intended to provide general information. Nothing substitutes for formal instruction, routine practice, and plenty of experience. When you follow any of the procedures described here, you assume responsibility for your own safety. Under normal conditions, excursions into the backcountry require attention to traffic, road and trail conditions, weather, terrain, the capabilities of your party, and other factors. Keeping informed on current conditions and exercising common sense are the keys to a safe, enjoyable outing.

—*The Mountaineers Books*

Conversions for Measuring Length

U.S.		Metric
1 inch		2.54 cm
1 foot	12 inches	0.3048 m
1 yard	3 feet	0.9144 m
1 mile	1760 yards	1.6093 km

- To convert inches to centimeters, multiply by 2.54.
- To convert centimeters to inches, multiply by 0.39.
- To convert feet to meters, multiply by 0.3.
- To convert meters to feet, multiply by 3.28.
- To convert yards to meters, multiply by 0.91.
- To convert meters to yards, multiply by 1.09.
- To convert miles to kilometers, multiply by 1.61.
- To convert kilometers to miles, multiply by 0.62.

Temperature Conversions

Fahrenheit	Celsius
0	-18
25	-4
32	0
45	7
50	10
60	15.5
75	24
80	27

- To convert Fahrenheit into Celsius, subtract 32 and multiply by 0.55.
- To convert Celsius into Fahrenheit, multiply by 1.8 and add 32.

Cooking Conversions

1/5 teaspoon = 1 ml
1 teaspoon = 5 ml
1 tablespoon = 15 ml
1 fluid oz. = 30 ml
1/5 cup = 50 ml
1 cup = 240 ml
2 cups (1 pint) = 470 ml
4 cups (1 quart) = .95 liter
4 quarts (1 gal.) = 3.8 liters

1 oz. = 28 grams
1 pound = 454 grams

16 tablespoons = 1 cup
12 tablespoons = 3/4 cup
10 tablespoons + 2 teaspoons = 2/3 cup
8 tablespoons = 1/2 cup
6 tablespoons = 3/8 cup
5 tablespoons + 1 teaspoon = 1/3 cup
4 tablespoons = 1/4 cup
2 tablespoons = 1/8 cup
2 tablespoons + 2 teaspoons = 1/6 cup
1 tablespoon = 1/16 cup
2 cups = 1 pint
2 pints = 1 quart
3 teaspoons = 1 tablespoon
48 teaspoons = 1 cup

- To convert ounces to grams, multiply by 28.35.
- To convert grams to ounces, multiply by 0.035.
- To convert pounds to kilograms, multiply by 0.45.
- To convert kilograms to pounds, multiply by 2.21.
- To convert gallons to liters, multiply by 3.79.
- To convert liters to gallons, multiply by 0.26.